My Beliefs — The Whole, Complete Truth
By: Katherine Horton - James

ISBN: 13:978-1507667002
10:1507667000

Table of Contents

Introduction

Recently on Red Flag News, there was an Article calling most Americans "Extremists." Well, I may be "Labeled" that, but the Real Truth is something entirely different. I wrote this Book specifically as a "push back" against a false Label. It is not a Crime to believe as I do, unless things have changed; thus I am unaware of the same. So listen closely and I will impart that which my Elders passed to me. I detest Politics, but this is something I simply cannot stay silent on. This is the final word on what I know to be true.

Allegedly, there are 32 counts against me, regardless of a Clean Background Check. I have done nothing except exercise my Legal Rights. I have been a good and decent citizen, doing my best not to do wrong. I try to run from trouble when and where I can. I am hardly scared and will fight where and when Applicable. Please read this with an open mind, as I mean no harm. This has forced me to treadmill repeat myself over and over again, answering the same Stupid items. I Hate to repeat myself.

My Beliefs

1.)   Yes, I do believe in Individual Liberties. I was raised Conservative. This is what my Ancestors fought for and believed in. This is the Burden I must also bear from their own Legacies. I believe in my Rights and Freedoms. My Late Maternal Grandfather Spoke regularly about these and other Topics.

2.)   Yes, I believe in States Rights. What I learned from my Elders, is that the States themselves have the Right to dictate and make their own Laws that will best Protect their own Citizens, that the Federal Government doesn't supercede State Laws. I was indeed taught that the Federal Government only have Legal Right where the Borders, Defense and Infrastructure are concerned.

3.)   Yes, I do want to make the world a better place. Don't we all? Isn't this the supreme purpose for which I and others are Incarnated here? Being a Tribal Elder and Senator for the Una Tribe of Mixed Bloods, I intend to improve Anglo and Native Relations. As a Medium, Author, Actress and Radio Host, I can improve the world through my healing work, bringing Peace, Healing and Closure to the lives of others.

4.)   Yes, my Ancestors are those who fought to free themselves from British Rule and who also wrote the Constitution and Bill of Rights. I will carry on their Legacy. It is my Genealogical Duty to do so.

5.) Yes, Communism is Never Ever a good thing. My own Ancestors, as recently as my own Grandparents, fought it and I will Refuse it and fight its influence on my own life. Communism shackles whole societies. If it doesn't stop, we will see a 3rd World War to obtain freedom. No one, I am certain, wants this.

6.) Yes, common sense says that the interests of my own Nation come before that of other Nations. I am not saying don't support or disagree with other Nations. By all means do so; but understand that our Nation comes first, with its People.

7.) Yes, being Female, I am clearly Anti - Muslim. I have seen and heard all the examples that I need to of what Islam does to women and girls. I don't need to know any more. They are a Death Cult.

8.) Yes, I know it for a Fact, that there will soon be a North American Union. I have seen many examples over many years. I am wide awake and opposed to the same.

9.) Yes, I am indeed opposed to a "New World Order." This is not a good thing either. It will only bring War, Death, Heartache and Destruction to the Globe.

10.) Yes, I am opposed to Agenda 21. I don't want nor agree with our Government Slaughtering its own People for Political Gain. It gets no one anywhere. it also expands Stalking Programs, of which I have been Targeted by myself.

11.) Yes, FEMA Camps do concern me. I cannot see anything but freedom for me and mine. I won't be immobilized, detained, isolated nor imprisoned. I will run if anyone tries.

12.) Yes, I do fear any law that strips me of any of my Constitutional Rights. I refuse to yield or submit.

13.) Yes, alike to my Ancestors, I am a sovereign citizen. No explanation needed.

14.) Yes, there is considerable hate and bias against me. The Menacing Stalking against my family and I proves this beyond any shred of doubt.

15.) Yes, I am indeed frustrated by mainstream ideologies. It just doesn't match who I am. It also leaves more questions than answers.

16.) Yes, I do indeed have a grievance. I was Stalked for up to 12 years. Why won't the Law do its Job and nab the Bastard?!

17.) Yes, I have just as much right to voice my opinions as anyone else, Bumper Stickers or no Bumper Stickers. I also have just as much right to my personal Patriotism as anyone else.

18.) Yes, I am fiercely Nationalistic, to an extent. Why shouldn't I be? I was Born and raised in this country.

19.) Yes, I am Anti Global. I Respect other Countries, but I will always believe in the greatness of the USA and its People.

20.) Yes, a Centralized Federal Authority is more dangerous than States taking care of their own.
It Promotes Communism. (See #5).

21.) Yes, I am Reverent of Individual Liberty. My Ancestors were and that is how I was raised; to believe that it is right. (See #1).

22.) Yes, my way of life is indeed under attack. I won't yield or submit to a life of Restricted Freedoms. I will run. (See #'s 14 and 16).

23.) Yes, I want Autonomy. I won't allow anything else.

24.) Yes, I am concerned about Illegal Immigration. My Ancestors came here Legally. So should everyone else. Illegal Immigration takes Jobs away from Americans, they bring Crime and possibly disease, which could potentially unfairly burden Americans.

25.) Yes, I believe in the Right to bear Arms. It is a Right written into the United States Constitution and it was fought for by my Ancestors.

26.) Yes, of course I fear a Communist Regime. I fear anything that would otherwise falsely imprison my family and I for any reason. (See #5).

27.) Yes, I am against Illegal Immigration. For the last time - my Ancestors came here legally. (See #24).

28.) Yes, for the last time - the NWO is wrong on many levels. I will not tolerate anything that in any way restricts my freedoms or that of my family. (See #9).

29.) Yes, I do Not like the UN because they want to overthrow US National Sovereignty. We as Americans, cannot allow this to happen.

30.) Yes, I will indeed support anyone who is Anti Obama. Obama has mostly destroyed the USA.

31.) Yes, I have the Legal Right to use the Gadsden Flag or any other Flag, within reason, as I see fit. No law against it.

32.) No, I am not a Bigot for Refusing and Rejecting Sharia Law. I simply oppose anything that will Falsely Enslave me. If Ms. Maxine Waters likes it so much, then why doesn't she herself convert to Islam? Then she might just have a leg to stand on.

33.) Yes, I am Pagan. I believe in Spirit, Past Lives, Karma, Shamanic Medicine, the Elders who built this Nation and in my Country. I believe in putting my heart and soul into everything that I do and work for.

34.) Yes, some of these Government Policies are Severe Over Reach and need to be done away with. Honestly, they are downright dumb and delusional.

35.) I do not agree with "Occupy" anything (unless it is my own home and life). It is not helping anything and is causing more trouble than solutions. I am at least, in agreement Morally, with the TEA Party.

36.) Taking Photos and Videos of what?! I honestly thought that was my Legal Right to do so.
37.) Yes, most of my closest friends and Associates are Police Officers. I Love them. I would give my life to Protect them.

38.) Yes, in certain and specific cases, I am against War, but in others, there is reason for it.
39.) Yes, I write all the time, whether on or off paper. I am an Author. That is what I do. Not a crime.

40.) Yes, I do value On Line Privacy. After everything my family and I have been through, I should value this. Myself and others should Not be spied upon by anyone, no matter who it is.

41.) Yes, I am at least "Anti - Tax," to a degree. I know and understand why certain Taxes exist and why they are necessary. Other Taxes (unless necessary), should be done away with. They are over reaching and useless, sometimes double and triple dipping.

42.) Yes, I search Google. At current time, I am House Hunting for a place for my family and I to live Permanently. I also use this for certain aspects of my work, as does my Husband.

43.) I have never been in the Military, but I deeply Respect the Military. Most of my Ancestors were in the Military.

44.) Yes, I Respect the Constitution. (See #12).

45.) Yes, I own Guns. It is my Legal, Constitutional Right to do so; to Protect against those who would harm my Home, Family and Possessions. I am not ashamed of it.

46.) Yes, I did not vote for Obama. But this does not make me a Terrorist of any kind. I simply Refused to acknowledge nor condone the Mud Slinging. No one got my vote. In Fact, I gave up Voting in Elections for President, because no Candidate would spell out what they would do for this Country.

47.) Yes, I buy up to one month's Groceries at a time. This is all that my current Income will allow me to buy. Not because I have any intentions of anything.

48.) Yes, I question Big Government. It is simply crazy. Why should Government Overwhelm this Nation? (See #'s 5 & 20).

49.) Yes, my Tap Water tastes horrible. I guess that is how Well Water is supposed to be.

50.) Yes, I am 39 years young. How in the Hell am I supposed to act?

50.) Yes, I am 39 years young. How in the Hell am I supposed to act?

51.) Yes, I use Social Media. So does everyone else.

52.) Yes, I eat using spices and they usually come out brightly colored.

53.) Yes, I used to be for the TEA Party; until I realized that they are all talk, no action on Government Misdeeds.

54.) Yes, I paid cash a couple times at an Internet Cafe, but only because I bought a bottle of juice. Not like I broke some freaking Law.

55.) Yes, I hold some Gold. Some dollar Coins are Gold. Everyone has them.

56.) Yes, I take Pictures and occasional Videos. So does everyone else.

57.) Yes, I talk to the Police whenever. They are a part of this Community.

58.) Yes, I wear a Hoodie. It is comfortable and to Promote my Business. Nothing illegal there.

59.) Yes, I write consistently on Paper. I take Notes, Journal and write Books. I am an Author.

60.) Yes, I am a Libertarian. What is anyone going to do to me about it Physically?

61.) Yes, I happen to be Partial to the Founding Fathers. They are my Biological Ancestors. Duh!

62.) Yes, I am for the Gold Standard. It is stable. 63.) Yes, I am opposed to Genetically Engineered Foods. I am Chemical Sensitive.

64.) Yes, I oppose Surveillance. I don't want to be watched 24/7. I am a Sovereign Citizen.

65.) Yes, I will do anything and everything to Protect my Privacy.

66.) Yes, I am a Southern Confederate Descendant. I believe in my Family, my Roots and my Lineage. Not a Crime.

I make NO Apologies for being Southern by Traced Direct Lineage! I make NO Apologies for Loving my Ancestors, same as anyone would their own. I am a Descendant of Southerners (Lineage Traced 16 Generations), as is my Husband on his Mom's side. Both of our Families were Confederates. Among my own Lineage, are Generals, Major Generals, Privates and 7 Soldiers who perished in Prison Camps of unimaginable, horrid diseases. Our families got lucky to have mostly survived the War years and come west. Many of mine though, turned Outlaw because of resentment that the Government wouldn't allow them to go straight after the War. So therefore, I keep a Confederate Flag in my Genealogy Room as a Tribute and Memorial to them. In Spirit, my Husband and I are very close to our Ancestors. This whole thing in Charleston NEVER should have happened. But the Confederate Flag has Nothing to do with this. Neither do Guns in general.

I am a Firearms Owner too. I have only needed mine a small handful of times to defend myself. However, Dylan Roof was also messed up at the time on drugs (No, Not an excuse of any kind). Drugs and Guns and Alcohol and Guns are a Bad Mix. Thank Goodness he is in custody. Hate has to be faced head on, but all this stuff with Flags and Guns is just a distraction from the Real Argument here - Destroying Hate. I have Black Ancestors and Cousins whom I personally Adore and would give my last breath for. Many of my friends and Associates are Black and of most all Nationalities, including Native American Ancestors, friends and Colleagues, whom I am Very close with. I Love beyond Color, Race, Creed and Nationality. It is organizations like the KKK that make us Real Southerners and Southern Descendants look bad. If anyone wants more info on Real Confederate History, I have Relations and Colleagues I can point ya'll to that are Fantastic Resources. They know far more than I do. But one thing is for certain; the War was Not over Slavery. It was over the Right of the States to fairly Govern themselves. The North wanted Control and the South said No. The North overstepped its bounds. I am a Proud Southern Descendant. Leave my Family's Heritage alone. I am also Not a "Dumb Hick." I am Self Educated. I hold 2 Masters' Degrees and want to get a PhD in Parapsychology. I own my own Business. I do stand with Charleston in their time of grief and Mourning. Love, Peace, Healing and Condolences to those who lost Loved Ones. Sending Big Hugs from NM.

Also, according to my Family's Records, the Federal Army overtook my GGG Grandparents' Plantation, used it for an HQ, then proceeded to loot it and burn it to the ground, while my GGG Grandmother and my GG Grandfather, with his Brothers and Sisters, as well as the Family's Employees watched in horror as their Home and final possessions were burned to the ground. Their fields were Torched, set ablaze. When my GGG Grandfather (a x3 Prison Camp Internee), returned home from the War, he found my GGG Grandmother and the Family, destitute, living in a Tent. They packed up and went West, managing by some Miracle, to rebuild their Fortune in Utah. On my Father's Father's Line, we know what happened to my GG Grandfather, Jesse James and his Family. Many more of my Ancestors who were Confederates, although being Major Generals, were killed Horrifically. Only General, my 9th Gr. Uncle, Robert E Lee, survived the War and died in his sleep. He was lucky. My Hubby's GGG Grandfather, Maj. Thomas Jefferson McQuiddy, was Confederate CIA. He came west to CA and made a name for himself there. This is all Truth. All of this is Direct Family Records. am Not Angry, other than sad about what happened in Charleston. But I am not pleased about erasing History. Erasing History means that as a People, we will fight ourselves to extinction, repeating the very Mistakes of the Ancestors. That is insane.

I believe in honoring Ancestors, Military Service, Home, Family and Life.
If any Media or Governances believe me and mine to be a Threat just for Heritage Rights, come and get us!
What have we ever done to you or anyone?!
We intend to buy and display our Confederate Flags and we won't be apologizing.
Unfreaking believable! A 1% Tax on me, mine and others, just for White Blood?!
F that! REVOLUTION - NOW!
Now I am not allowed to Decorate my Ancestors' Final Resting Places?!
WTF is with you, Gov?!
I won't stop doing that!
Oh, Hell NO!

Anyone - regardless of Gender, Race, Creed, Color or Religious Affiliation, comes up here, looking for Trouble, will receive Trouble in return.
We Own this place that we live. It is our Legal Right to Protect and Defend this piece of ground, even if by Deadly Force.
We want to live here in Peace and be left Alone.
We Did NOT come here to be Attacked and Abused by anyone - we are minding our own affairs.

Welfare? No. Don't believe in it.
I take care of my own.

Chipping? No. I am opposed to the same.
My body rejects all foreign objects.
It would likely kill me by Infection.

Because of all of this Garbage and abuse we have suffered, I am seriously considering moving my family and I to the Mountains of Scotland to escape all the Hell we have been through.

I am also incredibly Proud of Southerners for
standing up to NASCAR.
NAACP needs to leave the South alone and stop the
Nonsense.
Stop destroying our Monuments, renaming and
removing our Heritage.

I don't blame, but am incredibly Proud of those who
are guarding our Military Recruitment Centers.

Really, if the USA is going to have anothr go at
another Civil War, then we need to pull out of
funding any and all other Nations and we need to
pull out of all other foreign engagements too.

Unfortunately, the first shots have been fired in a
New Race War, that will touch off CW2.
People ar being killed over a piece of cloth.
I will be going South, with my Southern Relations.

Advisement for the "Black Lives Matter" People

First, let me open this with the Fact that you
created your own Problems.
Maybe this advisement can give you some pointers to
fix your demands and issues.

1.)   Don't act like Jackasses and Victims and
you won't get discrimination.

2.)   Police won't be brutal if you treat them
with Respect.
You are not actually "Oppressed." You put
yourselves in that position.

3.)   Go out and actively seek Employment.
No one actually owes you a living.
Better yet, take your life's Passion and build a
Business around it.
There is plenty of room for more Entrepreneurs.

4.)   Make an effort to physically revitalize
and build your communities.
You can end Class Warfare by building yourselves
up.

5.)   First, stop being Criminals.
Go to School. Get an Education.
Education is Free to all.
Don't tell me it isn't. It is.

6.)   Again, Stop being Criminals.
Be Educated and the Prison Complex will go away.
Raise children the right way, No Teen Pregnancy,
then this will disappear on its own.
Education is the Absolute Key to end this.

7.) The WH and the Government owes no one anything.
Get Educated, go into the Law Profession, or
register to Vote at age 18.
Get into the Political System.
Change the Law through Legal Means, instead of Law
breaking and Protesting.
The more you Protest, the less the Government will
listen.

8.) Go raise your own food. Learn Gardening
and open Community Gardens.
Otherwise, go search out healthy foods at the
Grocery Store.

9.) No one is disenfranchizing you. You are
doing this to yourself. As soon as you are of
age, get educated on Facts, Figures and
Issues. Go Vote and change things Legally. No
one owes it to you.

10.) You have Black History Month.
If you are unhappy with the way your History is
being taught, then Author, Write your own Books and
present them as teaching materials.

11.) On the issue of ridiculous demands, I
doubt very highly that the Government will
listen.
Letting out All Political Prisoners, could be
extremely dangerous. You may one day, come to
regret this.

12.) The Military is Not destroying Black and
Brown Communities. Yes, it did happen once, but
they have moved on from this.
You destroy yourselves through Protesting,
Demanding and acting like Criminals.

There is No "White Supremacist System."
Act like Thugs, get treated accordingly.

On Societal Politics

A Message to the President and First Lady:

First, Ovomit; you need to Arm our Military Recruiters and let them do their Jobs.
You also need to be Encouraging the wearing of their Uniforms instead of discouraging it.
Your Ovomitcare thing is a Joke and needs to be repealed.
We won't be buying into it.
You are Not a King nor a Dictator.
You are Not now, have Never been and will Never be my President.
I don't care what your Orientations are. Not my business nor my personal concern.
I care that your Policies are destroying this Nation.
You also need to Stop, Cease and Desist your Gun Bans.
You do this and I can guarantee you will see a 2nd American Revolution. You woke a sleeping giant.
Don't say I didn't warn you.
No one gave you Permission to railroad and Destroy the Constitution.
No more Voter Fraud, tearing down flags and Monuments nor being ok with all of this Garbage and Nonsense.
Cease ALL Foreign Aid to Nations who hate ours too.
Do you Not see that you are taking this Nation backward instead of forward?
Or is that your every intention?
And now everyone in this Nation are "Hate Groups?"
Please proceed to get a grip, get a life and get over yourselves.
Now the UN is superceeding our own Congress?!
Seriously?!
Do your job, Ovomit, or We The People will do it for you.

Oh, and I quadruple Dog Dare you to come to my own face and call me a Racist!
Just try to prove that I am.
You won't be able to.
I guarantee it.
I know you defy this Nation and its Laws.
You are an unjust coward.
Good on Montana for pulling out of your Lunch Program, Moochelle.

For the Muslims that think that they will take over:
Most likely, myself and most Americans will do just the opposite of what you will ban and do it just a bit more.

1.) Ok. I don't consume Alcohol at all, but this may just drive me to drinking.

2.) Pork. Well, this being a Southern Staple, will be used even more frequently.

3.) Gambling. I am a Blackjack Champ from way back. I may just start to playing again and bust Casino Houses.

4.) Porn. No comment.

5.) Usury. Nope. Let those who do that, do so to their hearts content.

6.) Promiscuity. Nope. Faithfully Married.

7.) Freemixing. Nope. Faithfully Married.

8.) Gays. Nope. Know some who are.

9.) Cinemas. Really?! I will go to those just to piss off the Universe.

19

10.) Idolatry. Looks like I will be doing this more, just to piss off the Universe.

11.) Insurance. Really?! I mean yes, it would save us some significant money over time, but is still one of those things that would just make the world go to Hell.

12.) Stocks and Shares. Geez... I guess I will have to learn how that is played and do it even more, just to piss off the Universe.

13.) Insulting Prophets. Really?! Ha! That is a hoot! Theirs has quite an unsavory background. They don't insult mine, I won't insult theirs.

On the Economic Collapse:

I am hardly surprised that Poverty is up.
Even my own family and I are struggling.

Thank Goodness that my family and I are now Homeowners. We still continue to struggle though.

I refuse Government Dependence.
I am on a Family Trust that I continue to try desperately to get off of, to no avail.

The National Debt needs desperately to be lowered.

Even our own belts have tightened as the Economy shrinks.

My own Business cannot get the word out. I have been essentially locked out of the Marketplace.

I finally stopped looking for work. I cannot even get Customers for my Business.

I do look for work daily, to no avail.

Screw China. Bring Jobs back to the USA.

Yeah, we "Middle Classers" have no future here in
the USA. I now consider me and mine to be "Lower
Class."

I myself have even seen total Economic Collapse
coming, but there is little or nothing can be done
to stop it from happening.

General Politics

I do believe that all Gun Stores should be Muslim Free. Especially after daily attacks.

No surprise there that Iran would defy the USA.

EPA needs to get lost and drop out of sight.

Trump is one for the Truth. I am with him on that.

WBC needs to sit down, shut up and stop their hateful Protests.

Wow! A Secret Menu at McD's! Perfect for my vow to eat myself stupid.

I am not surprised that Prison costs. Society as a whole costs.

Unbelievable! Seattle is trying to ban Land Ownership?!
It is now "Racist" to Own Land?! WTF?!

Good. Revoke the citizenship of all of those tied to Terror.

"Black Power?!" What about good old fashioned work togethr by All "Human Power?!"

Time to flush this Nation of ALL Illegals and good on the Law in FL for getting another Nasty No Good off the streets.

Sadly, the UK and Europe are screwed up worse than here. They could turn it all around if they really wanted to.

OMG! I know I am a Critter Squish, but the Libtards are out of control and WAY out of touch.

Cool! Stephen Hawking is looking for ET's.
Well, he can go after Robert "Todd" Sterling, who
claims to be an Evil Gray Alien.

Leae Gun Store Owners alone! They have the Legal
Right to decide what goes for their Businesses.

I do wholly agree, that School Staffs need to be
Armed to Protect their Students.
It is just common sense.

And as if things couldn't get any worse; Navajo
Nation is turning their backs on their own
Language?! WTF are my Cousins there thinking?!

WHAT?! Stone Mountain is going to be Destroyed?!
WTF?! Now it is WAR!

Love and Condolences to those gone from Police and
the other Brutalities of life. Nothing is in vain.

WTG, FL for Reinstating the Confederate Flag!
Heritage Not Hate!

Why release Criminals at all? They will just re
offend.

Another Holy Miracle. Late Psychic Medium Sylvia
Browne said it would happen.

Unfortunately No Presidential Candidate meets my
standards at this time.
I won't be Voting in the next Election.

Good on the Lady who took back her Late Hubby's
Truck from thieves. We Need more Brave Women like
her.

Here in NM, Criminals and bad or lazy cops are the Normal thing. You must do the Law's Job for it here.

Awesome! There is now a Saliva Test for Alzheimer's Disease.
It could save a lot of lives.
I hope that it goes forward.

Remember, folks; don't leave a child or a pet in a hot car.

Now New Americans don't have to Pledge to defend the USA?! WTF?! Talk about Cultural Cleansing! Before long, the USA will be nothing but a Door Mat!

No Country of Origin Labeling?! What next?! Heaven help our Nation!

Here is to ALL Veterans, here or in Spirit. Rest easy. You are Loved.

Butt Implants are trendy now?! No thanks. I think I will keep what I have Naturally.

Ok. I am not Christian. I am Pagan. I do support Freedom of Religion, but I am having more and more of an issue with Muslims.
Also, besides just Christians being under Attack, so are Amrican Values, as a whole.

Minimum Wage Hike for Fast Food?! UGH! Up goes Inflation!

Now Global Warming based on Isis formation?!
Stupidity is growing by the day.
Stupid is as Stupid does.

Fly the American and Confederate Flags both.
This Cultural and Heritage Cleansing is becoming sickening.

Yes, ALL Lives DO Matter! Get it straight!

Yes, Gun Free Zones do need to be banned.
They are indeed open invites for any manner of societal filth.

I do support Apache Stronghold fight for their Sacred Lands.

Feinstein needs to sit down, shut up and stop her blathering.

VA Hospitals need to get their stupid act together and start getting Veterans taken care of better.

HaHa! Silly Rodeo Bull. He went on the lam and got busted for it.

Yay to Kurdistan for Honoring our Troops.

I completely agree with Army Chief Odierno that the rise of Isis could well have been prevented. US Gov is Stupid.

On screaming babies and toddlers; I do know how to soothe them. I am a soft hearted Aunty after all.

Trump is an uneducated fool and idiot when it comes to the Confederate Flag.

Congrats Kyle Carpenter on receiving the Medal of Honor. I am Proud of you.

Sources

1. Those that talk about "individual liberties "
2. Those that advocate for states' rights
3. Those that want "to make the world a better place "
4. "The colonists who sought to free themselves from British rule"
5. Those that are interested in "defeating the Communists"
6. Those that believe "that the interests of one's own nation are separate from the interests of other nations or the common interest of all nations "
7. Anyone that holds a "political ideology that considers the state to be unnecessary, harmful, or undesirable"
8. Anyone that possesses an "intolerance toward other religions"
9. Those that "take action to fight against the exploitation of the environment and/or animals "
10. "Anti-Gay "
11. "Anti-Immigrant "
12. "Anti-Muslim "
13. "The Patriot Movement "
14. "Opposition to equal rights for gays and lesbians "
15. Members of the Family Research Council
16. Members of the American Family Association
17. Those that believe that Mexico, Canada and the United States "are secretly planning to merge into a European Union-like entity that will be known as the 'North American Union '"
18. Members of the American Border Patrol/American Patrol
19. Members of the Federation for American Immigration Reform

20. Members of the Tennessee Freedom Coalition
21. Members of the Christian Action Network
22. Anyone that is "opposed to the New World Order "
23. Anyone that is engaged in "conspiracy theorizing "
24. Anyone that is opposed to Agenda 21
25. Anyone that is concerned about FEMA camps
26. Anyone that "fears impending gun control or weapons confiscations "
27. The militia movement
28. The sovereign citizen movement
29. Those that "don't think they should have to pay taxes "
30. Anyone that "complains about bias "
31. Anyone that "believes in government conspiracies to the point of paranoia "
32. Anyone that "is frustrated with mainstream ideologies "
33. Anyone that "visits extremist websites/blogs "
34. Anyone that "establishes website/blog to display extremist views "
35. Anyone that "attends rallies for extremist causes "
36. Anyone that "exhibits extreme religious intolerance "
37. Anyone that "is personally connected with a grievance "
38. Anyone that "suddenly acquires weapons "
39. Anyone that "organizes protests inspired by extremist ideology "
40. "Militia or unorganized militia " 41. "General right-wing extremist "
42. Citizens that have "bumper stickers" that are patriotic or anti-U.N.
43. Those that refer to an "Army of God "

28

44.   Those that are "fiercely nationalistic (as opposed to universal and international in orientation) "

45. Those that are "anti-global "

46. Those that are "suspicious of centralized federal authority "

47. Those that are "reverent of individual liberty "

48. Those that "believe in conspiracy theories "

49.   Those that have "a belief that one's personal and/or national 'way of life' is under attack " 50. Those that possess "a belief in the need to be prepared for an attack either by participating in paramilitary preparations and training or survivalism "

51. Those that would "impose strict religious tenets or laws on society (fundamentalists) "

52. Those that would "insert religion into the political sphere "

53. Anyone that would "seek to politicize religion "

54. Those that have "supported political movements for autonomy "

55. Anyone that is "anti-abortion "

56. Anyone that is "anti-Catholic "

57. Anyone that is "anti-nuclear "

58. "Rightwing extremists"

59. "Returning veterans"

60. Those concerned about "illegal immigration"

61. Those that "believe in the right to bear arms "

62. Anyone that is engaged in "ammunition stockpiling "

63. Anyone that exhibits "fear of Communist regimes "

64. "Anti-abortion activists "

65.   Those that are against illegal immigration
66. Those that talk about "the New World Order"
in a "derogatory" manner
67. Those that have a negative view of the
United Nations
68. Those that are opposed "to the collection
of federal income taxes "
69. Those that supported former presidential
candidates Ron Paul, Chuck Baldwin and Bob Barr
70. Those that display the Gadsden Flag ("Don't
Tread On Me")
71. Those that believe in "end times"
prophecies
72. Evangelical Christians

Source: http://www.zerohedge.com/news/2015-01-
13/obama-declares-war-extremism-%E2%80%93are-you-
extremist

David R April 18, 2014

Labeling It's Own Citizens as Domestic Terrorists
The Ultimate Betrayal by the Federal Government
Read more at

http://freedomoutpost.com/2014/04/labeling-citizens-domestic-terrorists-ultimatebetrayal-federal-government/#z3aqA6WfsWAOdfGx.99

When a young man or woman joins the United States military, one of the first things they do before even being shipped off to boot camp is take the loyalty oath. "I (state your name) do solemnly swear to uphold and defend the Constitution of the United States of America against all enemies, foreign and domestic, and I will bear true faith and allegiance to the same." The oath of enlistment goes on to say that the service member will follow orders of the president and the officers appointed over them per the regulations of the uniformed code of military justice. Most service members, at least I hope anyway, understand that there are illegal orders, and any order that goes against the Constitution is, in fact, an illegal order. Read more at http://freedomoutpost.com/2014/04/labeling-citizens-domestic-terrorists-ultimatebetrayal-federal-government/#z3aqA6WfsWAOdfGx.99

This oath means something to military personnel because most of us joined to defend the rights and liberties of all Americans, even those that don't share our views. Sadly, many people have been inundated with the belief that the Constitution is an oppressive document that stands in the way of government creating the perfect paradise. In fact, in a report called Rightwing extremism: Current economic and political climate fueling resurgence in radicalization and recruitment the government calls anyone who refers to the Constitution and the limits of government power a domestic terrorist. Anyone who owns a gun is a terrorist, anyone who didn't vote for Obama is a racist terrorist and anyone who is buying more than seven days of food.

31

www.ingramcontent.com/pod-product-compliance
Lightning Source LLC
Chambersburg PA
CBHW081130280526
45787CB00007B/3038